Published by: Lillian Hammond

Disclaimer

By purchasing this book, you acknowledge that the ideas included are solely the opinions of the author and are for entertainment purposes only. You are responsible for your personal decisions and no part of this book should be considered as legal or professional advice.

Except where specifically acknowledged, the information included in this work is believed to be common knowledge obtained from many and varied sources. Whilst there has been no verbatim use of copy, it is possible that parts have been gleaned from publications and websites and this is gratefully acknowledged in the source section of this book.

Table of Contents

1. FOREWORD

First of all, I would like to congratulate you on your upcoming wedding!

Until I started organising my own wedding, I often wondered how people managed to spend tens of thousands of pounds on their wedding! My husband and I always wanted a very “chic” and classy wedding, without taking on any loans or using credit cards. We knew this was possible (how? We didn’t know yet) but we knew we had to make it happen. We were not prepared to spend £15,000 or more on our wedding. It took us about 6 months of intensive research to find out how we could save on our wedding costs. It is the fruit of this research that we wish to share with you.

My husband and I managed to organise the wedding of our dreams for £5000. I am now sharing the strategies I learnt, which have since been used by many people with success.

You will find many tips in this book, but if I were to give you one single advice, it would be to remember that this is your day, so make sure you do what you want for your wedding, not what is expected of you. By simply doing that you'll most probably make a number of savings!

Whether you are getting married this year, next year or in a few years time, this book is for you! It is packed with advice and tips that will help you save thousands of pounds.

To personalise this book, I have added comments based on how my husband and I organised our wedding. I am convinced that you will find this helpful.

Let me know how you get on. If you have any comments on the book or any ideas or tips that you would like to share, please e-mail me on contact@weddingforless.co.uk.

2. INTRODUCTION

It seems there are a couple of ways of looking at saving money for a wedding; either spending as little as possible or getting as much value for money as possible while not cutting back on much. This is what I would like to share with you.

There are 10 easy steps to planning your wedding.

- Step 1: Read our analysis of wedding costs
- Step 2: Agree wedding type with Fiancé(e)
- Step 3: Decide on wedding budget and set wedding date
- Step 4: Agree where funds will come from
- Step 5: Choose wedding items that you wish to include in your wedding
- Step 6: Read our savings tips
- Step 7: Decide on budget for each item
- Step 8: Purchase and negotiate where possible
- Step 9: Plan the wedding day itself
- Step 10: Arrange post wedding activities

You will notice that steps 4 and 7 can be done using the wedding manager tool, which can be purchased from: www.weddingforless.co.uk.

Please note that you do not have to purchase the wedding planning tool, if you do not want to, this book will provide you with all the information you require to save money on your wedding costs.

The advantage of the wedding planning tool is that it provides you with:

- Budget planner
- A guest list manager
- Checklist for the groom
- Checklist for the bride.

3. THE AVERAGE WEDDING

3.1 Research on the average wedding

The aim of this section is to give you an idea of how much people spend on a wedding on average. If you are reading this book, it is because you don't want to follow the same path as everyone else.

According to an article published on the daily mail, "The average cost of a UK wedding has topped more than £18500".

According to one BBC article, the father of the bride no longer has to dig into his pockets to pay. Only a third of weddings are now financed by dad - with more couples opting to take on the cost themselves.

Section 3.2 will explain how one can easily get carried away and keep spending.

By understanding the most costly items on your weddings list, your attention would be focused on which items create the best savings opportunities. I will then demonstrate in the subsequent sections how you can reduce the cost of these items, and how it is possible to have a great wedding without breaking the bank.

3.2 Most expensive items on the wedding list

Here are sample prices of some of the most expensive items on your wedding list. These are only examples and I will show you how to cut down these costs, so do not be too alarmed by the figures.

1. **Wedding Reception**: This depends on the nature of the venue and the number of guests attending, but we can estimate the cost to be between £2,000 and £5,000. This does not include the additional cost of the evening function and drinks!

   For example, if you want to have a traditional full wedding lunch for 100 guests, the cost per head could be £50, amounting to a total of £5,000. A less lavish buffet may only cost £20 per head, bringing the total down to £2000.

   Drinks – In addition to the food, there are drinks to consider and the evening party. Do you want to serve free drinks or have your guests pay for their own drinks? Don't forget there is also the cost of the champagne for the toast and wine at the table.

   If you have an evening function, with a buffet at £20 per head, this could cost an additional £2000 on top of the cost of your wedding reception.

2. **Honeymoon**: This could be an extravagant trip to the Mauritius Islands or a week in a nice cottage somewhere in the UK. The honeymoon would on average cost £2,000.

3. **Rings**: This will depend on the type of ring, but the price would typically range between £100 (for high street rings) to £25,000 for a custom designed ring.

4. **Wedding photographs**: Depending on the format of the photographs and the extras that the

photographer will offer, this might cost between £300 and £3,000.

5. **Wedding Dress**: The cost of the dress may range from £500 upwards. Designer dresses could cost in excess of a £1000. A research by Mintel showed that the average wedding dress costs £826.

6. **Groom's wedding day outfit**: A morning suit might cost up to £600. This may not include the costs of the trousers, shirt and shoes.

7. **Wedding video**: From £500 upward. This can go up to £2000 in some cases, for example, if you want a DVD made for the whole day, with two or more professional videographers, plus extra footage.

8. **Wedding cake**: A four-tier cake can cost upwards of £400.

9. **Wedding car-hire**: This might depend on the length of travel and the type of car involved but the price of hiring one car for three hours will be from £250 upwards.

10. **Flowers**: Bridal bouquets from £50 upwards and buttonholes are £3 to £5 each. You also need to include table arrangements and church decorations which could total £150 or more.

11. **Presents**: You may want to offer presents to the bridesmaid, groom's mother, pageboys, best man, and bride's mother. The cost will vary depending on the present.

But remember, your wedding can cost a great deal more or a great deal less depending upon your budget, priorities and whether you use professionals or get family and friends to help out.

None of this includes the cost of other extras such as the stag and hen night, accommodation costs for some guests or evening entertainment.

That is why it is essential to define a wedding budget to monitor and control your costs throughout your wedding preparations. This takes us to the next section of our book which is all about agreeing the type of wedding you want to have.

4. AGREE ON YOUR DESIRED TYPE OF WEDDING

4.1 Discuss desired wedding with fiancé(e)

Before you can start with the budgeting of your wedding, you will need to sit down with your fiancé, and go through a number of questions together. You need to be clear from the start as to the type of wedding that both you and your other-half want to organise.

Talk to your spouse-to-be about what kind of wedding you both want. Discuss what kind of flowers, colours, venues, clothing, invitations, music and food you prefer.

Agreeing on the type of wedding that you want upfront will help you focus on where you will need to spend more and where you could make savings.

Now you will need to sit your fiancé(e) down and go through the following questions:

- What type of wedding do you want? (Church wedding, registrar, a blessing?)
- Where do you want to have your wedding? Some people choose to have a wedding abroad with very few family members.
- What type of dress and tuxedo would you wear? Would you be prepared to hire them, if necessary?
- Do you want to plan your wedding yourself or you do need help from others? If so, who would you like to get involved?
- How many people would you like to invite?

- What kind of flowers would you like? Where would you like them?
- Would you like to have bridesmaids, flower girls and pageboys?
- Do you want a wedding lunch and evening reception, or just one of these two?
- What type of food would you like to serve?
- Where do you want to have the reception? (Pub, home, restaurant, hotel?)
- Do you want to have some dancing? A band?
- What type of entertainment would you like for your wedding?
- What are the things that you can compromise on? For e.g. would you go for a less expensive dress but have a fabulous honeymoon?
- Is the most important item the reception venue and the meal or your wedding dress?
- Do you want to go on honeymoon?
- What type of honeymoon do you want? Do you want a trip to the Maldives or a nice week in Scotland or somewhere in England and Wales or Europe?
- Do you want your guests to enjoy free drinks from the bar or are you happy just to pay for the table wine and champagne?
- If you both have large families and many friends, do you want as many of them as possible to attend?

- How important are the photographs or video? Would you like to have them done professionally or are you happy to entrust this responsibility to your family and friends?

- How about the sitting arrangements? Do you want people to sit wherever they want, or do you want to have a pre-defined sitting arrangement?

- Will you need transport between the church/registrar and the reception venue? If so, what type of car would you like? Would you like to hire a car with chauffeur or would you prefer a friend drove you to the reception venue?

4.2 Review list of wedding items

Agreeing with your fiancé on the type of wedding that you want is the first step to agreeing on your priorities.

The next step is to go through the list of wedding items which you can find below and decide what items you need to purchase and those you are going to ignore.

You will then need to allocate how much you are prepared to put down for each item. In order for you to make an informed decision on the cost, I have provided in this section, tips that will help you save money.

Wedding Clothing
Wedding dress
Wedding headdress
Wedding shoes

Wedding Clothing
Wedding lingerie
Wedding jewellery
Bridesmaids' dresses and accessories
Page boy outfits
Ushers' outfits
Groom's outfit
Best man's outfit
Bride's parent's outfits
Groom's parent's outfits
Bride's going-away outfit
Groom's going-away outfit
Bridal Beauty
Hairdresser
Make-up
Beautician
Transport
To ceremony for bride, bride's father, bridesmaids and bride's mother
To ceremony for groom and best man
From ceremony to reception
From reception for bride and groom
Decorations (ribbons) for wedding transportation
Photography/Videography
Photography package
Videography package
Photograph album
Additional prints/videos
Flowers
Church
Reception
Bride's and bridesmaids' bouquets
Buttonholes for participants and guests

Wedding Clothing
Civil/Religious Ceremony Fees
Church, including bells, choir, organist and heating if required
Register office or Approved Premise fees including giving notice, certificate of marriage and the service
Reception
Venue hire
No. of People
Cost of meal(per head)
Balloons and decorations
Toastmaster
Wedding cake
Cake stand
Cake knife
Catering and equipment
Bridal favours
Drinks with meal, for toasts and evening
Arrival drinks
Entertainment
Honeymoon
Passports and visas
Travel
Accommodation
Bride's clothing
Groom's clothing
Spending money
Travel insurance
Inoculations
Stationery
Invitations and postage
Order of Service
Menus

Wedding Clothing
Place name cards and seating plan chart
Other personalised items such as napkins, coasters and matches
Thank-you notepaper
Gifts
Wedding ring for bride
Wedding ring for groom
Present for bride, bridesmaids, pages, ushers and best man
Present for groom
Present for bride's parents
Presents for newly weds
Other
Engagement party
Hen night
Stag night
Wedding co-ordinator fees
Wedding night venue, if not the honeymoon destination
Wedding insurance
Overnight accommodation for close family if required
Press announcements for engagement

5. BUDGETING FOR YOUR WEDDING

5.1 Why Budget?

You have now identified what type of wedding you would like. The next step is to develop a budget that you will stick to.

Budgeting for your wedding means defining a list of wedding items and deciding on how much you will spend on each of these items. This budget will help you control and monitor your expenses, and track where you have overspent and where you have made a saving. Unless you have access to unlimited funds, you will have to financially plan your wedding very carefully.

Most couples change their mind many times over how much they are willing to spend on any given item. By recording any changes to your budget, you will always be aware of the impact on the total cost. This will offer you the opportunity to adjust your expenditure levels accordingly.

For example, if you had budgeted £500 for a photographer, but found one that would charge you £300, you would have made a £200 savings. With a budget you can track such variances and decide whether you want to keep this as a saving or spend that extra £200 on something else.

Unfortunately, dealing with the financial aspects of wedding can be the cause of much tension between those involved in organising your wedding. However, by carefully monitoring and controlling your expenditure with the use of a budget, you will go a long way to reducing the stress often experienced during wedding preparations.

5.2 Mobilising the funds

Whether you, your parents or a combination of you and your parents are paying for your wedding, there will probably be a maximum of what each of you can afford.

You now need to agree on a budget (maximum amount you are willing to spend on your wedding) and commit to sticking to it.

At this stage, you should allocate a provisional sum for the total cost of your wedding. If you are paying for your wedding yourselves, only you have to decide on an approximate sum that you are prepared to spend. By paying for your own wedding, you will have more control over what happens and also who to invite (i.e. the budget and number of guests).

If the parents of the bride or groom are paying, or contributing, you will need to know what they are prepared to pay. However, many parents will ask for an estimate of the total cost of the wedding. With this information, they can then decide whether they can afford to pay all the costs as per the UK traditional responsibilities or decide on a sum they can afford.

You have to calculate how much money you currently have, how much you think you will need and how much you will have to save. Make a plan to save what you need, you may want to use a savings account specifically set up for your wedding.

My Experience

<u>Budgeting:</u>

My husband and I always knew we wanted to have a classy wedding without breaking the bank. We were adamant that we would not spend more than £5000. We talked through a number of options, including a wedding abroad, a blessing, or a wedding reception at home.

Agreeing on the type of wedding we wanted:

We wanted to have a nice meal with family and close friends (maximum 50 people) in a lovely location. We wanted our photographs to be done professionally but were happy to have friends take the video.

We decided on having the wedding in a nearby church and the reception in a hotel. We decided that we would only have one meal in the day (after the church ceremony).

Mobilizing the funds:

We decided to pay for our own wedding ourselves, so we agreed on putting money aside each month towards the cost of the wedding. In addition our parents also made a contribution which helped a lot!

Deciding on the budget:

The maximum amount we were prepared to spend on the wedding was £5,000.

5.3 Keeping your costs low

Using the money savings tips provided in this section, your task is to go through the list provided the section above and allocate a fixed sum for each item.

5.3.1 Harness the Talents of Family and Friends

Consider skills like design and floristry as well as extra drivers, first-aiders and photographers. Encourage talented musicians, speakers, hairdressers, make-up artists and cake makers to play a part. For example, you could have a close family or friend, be the chauffeur for the day.

Do not be afraid to inform those close to you that you are looking for ways to keep your wedding budget under control. They may offer their own skills to help you save money, or they may know how to help you find a great deal.

My Experience

Harnessing the talents of family and friends

My husband and I started going through a list of all our friends, and asked ourselves:

Who has a nice car? Who could do my hair and make-up? Who sings well (for the choir or soloist)? Who knows a photographer?

A friend of mine is a hairdresser so she did my hair for a minimal fee. My brother is part of a choir, so he did some of the singing. One of our friends is very good with taking videos, so we tasked him with the videography for the day.

5.3.2 Choose your wedding date

Once you have decided on your budget and the funding and have identified the amount you are willing to put aside for the wedding and how long it will take you to do so, you are now in a position to choose a date for your wedding.

Most people would usually set their dates before looking at how much funds they have or how much time it will take them mobilise these funds.

If you have not set your date yet, I would suggest going through the process I have just described.

By choosing the right date and time for your wedding, you could be in a stronger position to negotiate discounts and good prices.

❖ *Schedule Your Wedding "Off-Season"*

Nearly 70% of all weddings take place in May through October of each year. Even in matters of love, the laws of supply and demand apply. You will probably find yourself able to get better deals on virtually every wedding service if you schedule your wedding in one of the "off season" months.

You may want to avoid late November through the New Year, when hotels, caterers and bands are likely to be busy with holiday parties. What is the best time then?

You may consider setting your wedding date between **October and mid-November** and between **January and May** (avoiding Valentine's Day).

❖ *Schedule Your Wedding on a Week Day*

Obviously weekends are at a premium, and you can add on that little bit more in the summer months as well. Decide how important a weekend wedding is - in most cases it can't be avoided, but it will have a significant effect on your budget when you realise how venues, photographers, car hire, all have increased prices for these prime days.

Consider having your wedding any day but Saturday. Fridays are also popular wedding days and may cost a lot less than a Saturday event. For even greater savings, choose a weekday evening for your wedding. Schedule the wedding to allow guests, time to arrive at the ceremony after the workday has ended. Many guests enjoy weekday weddings as this frees up their weekends for other activities.

❖ *Consider Having Only One Function on the Day*

You can decide to have the wedding lunch with no evening party. This will save you on the evening meal.

❖ *Consider Afternoon Tea After The Ceremony.*

You could also organise a tea party instead of a sit down meal after the ceremony.

❖ *Set the Time For Late In the Day*

If you have the wedding ceremony late in the day, you will only need to have one meal and this could be an evening buffet.

❖ *Set the Time For Early In the Day*

Although I said earlier on, that you could save by having your wedding late in the day, likewise, you could save if you have it early in the day. You could have a beautiful morning brunch, which could be cheaper.

❖ *Choose an Unusual Date*

If you have a sense of humour and are not superstitious, you could pick April the 1st or Friday the 13th as wedding dates. These dates are obviously not very popular and you could get huge discounts!

My Experience

Choosing the wedding date and time

The wedding was scheduled for the 26th of November. This is in the low season and we found ourselves in a fantastic bargaining position as we negotiated on basically everything.

When setting the date we also considered how long it would take us to save for our wedding costs.

My husband and I decided to have a church wedding with the ceremony starting at 11.00 pm. We agreed that we would have the wedding lunch starting at 2.00 pm and then everyone will move to the hotel bar from 6.00 pm. This worked out very well, as after the sit-down meal, the cake and the speeches, everyone moved to the bar.

5.3.3 The venue

The venue and reception are areas where typically most of your costs will go. Depending on the venue, you would incur the following expenses:

- Site fee (i.e. fee for hiring the venue. This will depend on the type of venue – some venues would not charge you a site fee.)
- Cost of meal
- Cost of drinks

Your choice of venue is crucially linked to the final cost of your wedding. Venues range from castles (around £10,000 per day) to your favourite restaurant (probably just the food and drinks bill). Remember that many venues tie you to their own caterers, florists and bar charges. See appendix D for questions for the venue.

If you decide on a hall, you will need to find caterers - See appendix E for questions to ask the caterer.

Be wary of hidden costs like corkage, staffing and table decorations. For example, for corkage fees, you could be allowed to bring your own wines and champagne, but the venue may charge you a fee for opening each bottle.

Here are a few ideas for reducing your costs in this area.

- *Have Your Ceremony and Reception in the same place*

There will be no need for limousines to take you from one location to the other. Many houses of worship have halls that are equipped to handle wedding receptions at reasonable fees, especially if you are a member. Likewise, if you are having a civil ceremony, many venues have got a hall, where you could hold the reception. By doing that, you will not need to provide for arrival drinks, as this is often bought for people while they are waiting for everyone to arrive.

- *Find a Low-Cost Location*

If you're flexible about the "where" you can save a lot on your location. If you or your parents are members of a particular church, the location fee will probably be waived. A city-owned location, such as a public garden or historic building, may be available for a surprisingly low fee. And you might consider marrying at home (yours, or a friend with a big house), if your guest list isn't too large.

- *Hotel Reception*

If you are having your wedding in a low season, you will be in a better position to negotiate. When planning your ceremony and reception at a hotel, ask to speak to a manager who is in charge of these services. A manager should be in a position to offer the best rates for the hotel's services. Ask the manager to throw in extras. Hotels and catering halls have their own centrepieces that they are happy to loan. You should negotiate with the hotel to bring your own drinks and not be charged for corkage. Do not hesitate to tell the manager what your budget is and ask him/her what they can offer for the amount that you are prepared to pay.

- *Friend's or A Relative's House*

If you have a friend or relative who has got a big house with a nice garden, you could hold the reception at their house. You can hire a marquee and get caterers for a nice reception. For drinks you can take advantage of cheap drink offers from major supermarkets.

- *Hire a Hall*

There are many pretty halls that you can hire and which may require little decoration. They can cost from £10 per hour, but the cost will vary greatly depending on the location and the type of hall. If you choose to hire a hall, you will need to get caterers to provide the food, or ask a friend (preferably a cook) to prepare the food.

To find a hall, visit the website of the council where you want to marry and search for hall hires. You should be able to find something there.

To find caterers, you can follow this link:

- www.findaweddingsupplier.co.uk
- www.confetti.co.uk/confetti_pages/default.asp

❖ *Select Your Local Pub*

Your local pub may offer a sit down meal for £15-£20 a head. You will not have to worry about getting caterers and the pub may require minimal decorations or may even offer to help with the decorations. If you know the owner well, he may even give you a little extra.

❖ *Select Your Favourite Restaurant*

You can choose to hire your favourite restaurant for the wedding lunch. This is a good option as it may be cheaper than a hotel restaurant. Check www.toptable.co.uk for good restaurants.

❖ *Select a Venue That Does Not Charge a Hiring Fee*

Some pubs or restaurants would not charge you a site fee, so you could save on that wedding item by selecting such places.

❖ *Finding a wedding venue*

Here are links to finding wedding venues:

- www.wedding-venues.co.uk
- www.confetti.co.uk/venues/default.asp
- www.venues.org.uk/searches/wedding_venues.asp
- www.hitched.co.uk/venues/index.asp

5.3.4 Food and Drinks

The bill for food and drinks usually accounts for a huge chunk of your wedding costs. Here are some ideas about reducing your food and drinks bill.

- *Cut Down Your Guest list*

It may be painful, but the simple truth is that there is no quicker, easier way to control your budget than by limiting the size of the event. Again, your single biggest cost will be reception food and alcohol, so you can reduce that expenditure by reducing the number of people to invite.

This is difficult but sometimes necessary if the cost per guest is going to break your budget. Think of inviting only relatives with whom you have a close relationship instead of everyone related to you. To reduce the cost, you could invite only the people who are important to you and your parents rather than everybody you know.

- *Allocate a Specific Number of Guests to Both Sets of Parents*

The best way to do this is to draw up your own list as above and then allocate 'x' number of people to each set of parents. Let them make the hard decisions, which will take the strain off you. Don't forget, for your sanity, if you have any family members you most definitely do not want to invite, discuss this with your parents when giving them their list to fill. It's always better to be open and honest from the outset.

- *You do not have to pay For The Bar*

By all means buy the champagne, wine and soft drinks during the meal, but guests would fully understand that you can't be expected to pay for everything, if you do not pay for the drinks at the bar. Alternatively, you could put a tap behind the bar, for a specific amount. After this amount has been reached, the guests would pay for their own drinks.

- *Buy Your Own Soft Drinks and Alcohol*

Ordering from an online supermarket means cases can be delivered straight to your venue. If you bring your own drinks to the venue, you might be charged for corkage, please check this with the Manager.

- *Negotiate With the Chef*

Whether you are having the wedding lunch in a restaurant or in a hotel, there is always room for negotiation. If there is a given price for the wedding menu, you can get that reduced by speaking to the chef and asking him what he can provide for a cheaper price a head, based on your budget. You will often find that the alternative menu is as good as the more expensive one.

My Experience

<u>Our guests:</u>

When we first listed all the people that we wanted to invite, we had 100 people. Then we settled on the following criteria: anyone we are frequently in touch with or would like to invite to our marriage. This is how we eventually settled on the figure 40 (i.e. 20 from each side).

Coincidently, the hotel restaurant we picked could not accommodate more than 45 people (Great!). We had to stick to this number.

Looking back, we would not have done anything differently. The next day, we were not wondering how we would repay our costs for the wedding, we could fully enjoy our honeymoon and we had a memorable and very lovely day.

Food and drinks:

When we found the location of our dreams, we knew we had to get married there. It was just so beautiful. However, when we asked about the set menu for the wedding lunch, we were told it would cost £80 per person (including arrival drinks, four course meal, and wine with the meal).

There was no way we would pay £80 per head, so we told the banquet manager at the hotel, that the price we had in mind was around £30-35 per person maximum.

We wanted to invite a small number of guests so we did not mind spending on the meal, but our top price was £30 per head.

The banquet manager told us the alternative would be to have the restaurant on a private dinning deal, i.e. the meal would cost £35 and we will need to pay for the drinks ourselves. We asked him to speak to the chef and ask him what he could offer for £30 (instead of £35). The chef got back to us with 2 different menus and we chose the one we preferred.

The meal turned out to be excellent (costing us £30 per head).

We were in a strong bargaining position because we set our wedding date at the low season.

5.3.5 Music

Here are a few tips for cutting down costs:

- Have a DJ instead of a live band.
- You can get a number of CDs put together by a friend and play the songs on the CD player at the venue or restaurant.

- Use the talents of friends and family. If you know any pianist, DJ or soloist, this will come useful.

- Some pubs will provide the DJ for free. You will need to check with them.

My Experience

Reception music

For the music, my cousin made about 4 CDs, which we played during the reception at the restaurant. All went very smoothly and we did not need a DJ. We chose not to have dancing on the day, but more background music, which fitted the type of wedding we wanted.

5.3.6 The wedding cake

You do not need to have your wedding cake specially made for you. This will typically cost you in excess of £400. Major superstores now offer wedding cakes for much cheaper, and all you will have to do is decorate it yourself or get a florist to add flowers to the cake.

Here are your options which will cost between £25 and £75. You just need to buy the wedding cake and ask a florist to decorate it.

- **Marks & Spencer Cake**. You can buy a 3-tier wedding cake from Marks & Spencer's. You can then get a florist to decorate it with flowers.

- **Asda cake**. Asda has introduced a new wedding range. Here is the link to asda: www.asda.co.uk

- **Tesco cake**. You can buy a 3-tier wedding cake from Tesco on: www.tesco.com and search for cake).

If you wish to taste the cake, you can buy the smallest cake and taste it for yourself before buying the 3 or 4-tier cake.

Another option to cutting down your costs is to make your cake the dessert and cut the costs of the third course.

If you decide to buy your wedding cake from a superstore, you can use cake toppers from this website: http://www.charactercreations.co.uk

My Experience

Wedding cake

We got our wedding cake from Marks and Spencer, a 3-tier ivory fruit-cake for £64. We bought 2 sets of cake stands from Marks & Spencer. We had the cake decorated by the florist and this cost us an additional £40. The cake looked fantastic and tasted really good too.

Below is a picture of the cake we got from Marks & Spencer's, with flowers as decoration.

5.3.7 Bridal party

To cut down on your costs, you can choose to have only one bridesmaid, without flower girls or page boys. This will greatly depend on how important this is for you.

You would normally pay for the costs of their dresses, but depending on your relationship with them, they may be willing to pay for the dresses and shoes themselves. Your bridesmaids can also save money if you choose the colour but let them shop for a dress they like.

Here are a few options to purchasing dresses for your bridesmaids and flower girls or page boys:

- If your bridesmaids are young children, you could try shops like www.redoute.co.uk or www.vertbaudet.co.uk

- If bridesmaids are older just go round all the usual clothes shops and check out evening wear and party wear. For example, Monsoon, Debenhams, John Lewis, Coast, House of Fraser, Marks and Spencer and BHS.

My Experience

Bridal party

I only had one bridesmaid. We did not worry too much about the colour scheme and I let her choose whatever she wanted to wear on the day. I know this was pretty unconventional!

5.3.8 The wedding dress

You do not have to wear a designer dress that will cost you in excess of £1000. Keep in mind that once the wedding is over, the dress will be hanged in your room (or in the attic) unless you sell it. Here are a few ideas for reducing the cost of your wedding dress.

- *Hire the Wedding Dress*

Hiring a dress, including alterations, costs around £200 compared to the average cost of £826 for a wedding dress.

- *Select A Non-Bridal Gown*

You may find a non-bridal gown in the evening gown sections of stores like debehams, Coast, John Lewis.

- *Buy your dress second hand*

If you do not mind purchasing a second-hand dress, here are a few ideas for you. Check out the second-hand shops and scan the adverts in the papers for a wedding dress, and you may save considerably. Oxfam have got bridal shops, but in specific areas only. You can go onto their website and do a search for wedding dresses: www.oxfam.co.uk

Here are a few websites from people who are reselling their second hand wedding dresses:

- www.sharethedream.co.uk
- www.almostnewweddingdresses.co.uk

- *Try Confetti Warehouse Sale*

Confetti's website, would sometimes advertise warehouse sales. If you find a dress there that is too big for you, you can always take it and ask a seamstress to take it in for you. Go to: www.confetti.co.uk to find out the next warehouse sale.

- *Buy the Dress on Sale*

You could buy your wedding dress on sale. It may not be this season's wedding dress, but if you do not mind, it will cost you far less.

- *Have Your Wedding Dress Made*

You can have your dress made. The best way to find a dressmaker is to check your local Yellow Pages, or to follow this link: http://www.yell.com

My Experience

My wedding dress

My wedding dress was a non-bridal gown. It was purchased from Coast, during the sales, and was reduced from £300 to £60 (bustier and skirt). I got so many compliments on my dress, and I only bought it for £60. The quality was amazing and everyone thought it was a wedding dress.

5.3.9 Bridal beauty

Getting a make-up artist to do your make up on the day would cost from £150 to £500. Having your hair done on the day, could be about the same price.

There are ways to cut down on these costs...

- *Make Up*

  - **Get a make-over!** Go to department stores and have them give you a free make-over. If you like the products they use you may even buy them.

  - **Have a friend make you up.** Do you know of any friend, who is really good at making up? You can get her to do your make up or teach you how to make up? Have fun! Try different colours until you find the colours that you like.

- *Hair*

  - **Get your hair done professionally**. For your hair, I would advise getting it professionally done, preferably on the day. You can get a hairdresser to come to your house on the day to do your hair.

  - Get ideas for hairstyles through magazines or on the Internet. Check the following website: http://www.weddinghair.com or http://www.youandyourwedding.co.uk

You could try Google images to get ideas for your hair; you can do different types of searches by adding "short hair", "long hair" for example. To do that, go unto Google, select Images, and type in "wedding hairstyle".

My Experience

My hair and make-up

I had my hair done professionally by one of my friends who is a hairdresser. This was done on the morning of the wedding. I decided to do my make-up myself. As I can be quite difficult in terms of colours, lipstick, I thought it would be best if I did my own makeup. To learn how to apply make up well, I went to department store where I asked one of the make-up artist at a stand to make me up with their products, which I purchased.

5.3.10 Accessories

Accessories would include the veil, shoes, necklaces, shoes, earrings and bride's trousseau. The tiara can cost between £80 to £150, the veil would range from £100-£150 and the shoes, in excess of £80.

- *Tiara and Veil*

Is there anyone you could borrow the tiara from? If not, here are a few sites or ideas that will help you find the right tiara or veil for a fraction of the price.

- There are many places where you could buy your tiara for less. You can buy it from EBay or from big department stores such as BHS. Here are some links:
    - www.bhs.co.uk
    - www.ebay.co.uk

- *Shoes*

- You may find white/ivory shoes from any major shoe shop or department store. It will not necessarily be in their bridal section.

- *Jewellery and Bride's Trousseau*

- I would suggest Accessorize or any other shop where you can buy jewellery.

My Experience

Wedding accessories

I borrowed the tiara from my sister in law who got married a year before. I got my jewellery and trousseau from Marks and Spencer. Finally I bought my shoes on sale for £45 (and they were not bridal shoes), they are ivory high-heeled shoes that I can definitely wear again!

5.3.11 Groom's attire

It is always tempting to purchase the suit, but you could save much more by simply hiring it. You do not have to buy the suit unless you want to wear it again for another occasion.

You may want to hire it, this will cost you around £65 instead of £150 or more for a new suit.

There are a number of stores where you could rent your suit for a reasonable price:

- Moss Bros: www.mossbroshire.co.uk
- Young's: www.youngs-hire.co.uk
- www.hire-society.com

My Experience

My husband was the only one who hired a suit (for £64). My dad, my husband's dad and the best man wore their own suits.

5.3.12 Wedding rings

A popular place to buy rings is Hatton Garden near Holborn in London. It is a street full of jewellers. Depending on the ring, you can get a good price although personalized rings tend to be more expensive.

There are many other inexpensive alternatives:

- Argos does wedding rings which are quite affordable. Follow the link below and do a search for rings : http://www.argos.co.uk

- If you fancy making your own wedding rings you could try the wedding ring workshop on www.weddingringworkshop.co.uk . It is not cheap though!

My Experience

We bought our rings from Hatton Garden in London. They have many jewellery shops. As this was important to us, I had mine customised and my husband bought his off-the-shelf.

5.3.13 Decorations

You will need to decorate the church and the reception venue. The most strategic way to decorate is to pick a location that needs little or no embellishment.

❖ *Selecting Your Flowers*

- **Select flowers that are in season and locally available.** If you do, you'll probably find you can save considerably on cost, especially if you let your florist know that you are trying to keep your wedding costs low.

- **Find a flower wholesaler.** You can look in the Yellow Pages for a local flower wholesaler rather than paying full price from the florist.

- **Go to a flower market.** A flower market is where florists get their flowers from and you are allowed to buy there too. If you have talented friends in this area you can go with them to a flower market and get your flowers cheaply.

- **In-store florists:** Some stores have got in-store florist. You can get flowers for your bouquets and baskets of flowers made up (for flower girls). This will be much cheaper than getting them from your local florist shop.

- **Share the costs of the Church flowers.** If you're getting married in church sometimes you can arrange with other couples getting married on the same day to share the cost of decorating the church.

- **Try your local garden centre or even DIY store**.

- **Shop around**. Shop around at your local florists, get quotes and negotiate if you get a better deal in one shop, but like the other better. See section 6.1 on negotiating.

My Experience

The restaurant where we had our reception needed very little decoration. They provided bud flowers in vases on each table (at no extra cost for us, as this is what they normally have on tables). We did specify the colour scheme so that they could get us the right flowers.

Here is the break down for our flowers:

- Flowers for church: £60
- Cake: £40
- Bride's bouquet :£47
- Bridesmaid's bouquet: £30
- 4 Rosettes: (£4 each)= £16

5.3.14 Stationery

Stationery covers items such as invitations, "thank you" cards, order of service, name-tags, menu cards and guest book. There are many ways to save on stationary, you can either make your own stationary or buy your stationary at cheaper places.

❖ *Create Your Own Stationary*

- Create your own gorgeous stationery using a PC and digital camera. That way, one hundred invitations, menus and orders of service could cost you very little. Argos now sells DIY stationary kits or you could go to the likes of Hobbycraft.
- To create your own stationery, try the Paper Mill Shop for card, paper and many more: http://www.thepapermillshop.co.uk
- Other useful websites are:
  - http://www.weddingcrafter.co.uk
  - http://www.madaboutcards.com
- You can create your own order of service (using your computer) and get it printed professionally on nice paper.

❖ *Alternatively You Can Buy Your Stationery*

- If you prefer buying your stationery, here are a few ideas. You can find wedding invitations, "thank you" cards, from WHSmith or Clintons. Wedding invitations would cost you on average about £2 and £5 per card, whereas, you will pay £4.99 for 6 cards at Clintons.

- You can download an image you like and then get a quote from a local print shop for printing photographic cards. Alternatively, you could use the image to create your own stationery. You can find very lovely pictures on this link: www.istockphoto.com

My Experience

We got our wedding invitations from Clintons. The name tags and menus were complimentary from the hotel. We found a local company on the Yellow Pages that did our order of services for £2 per order of service.

5.3.15 Photographs

When selecting your photographer, do ask to view their portfolio of wedding pictures. Look for a photographer who captures sharp, expressive portraits combined with excellent communication skills to organise large groups.

Please note that in addition to the pictures taken, the photographer may charge you for giving you the pictures on a CD. This could add up approximately £150 to your cost.

There are many ways to reduce the price; here are a few tips:

- Hire the photographer for just a short period of time to take the formal pictures. Then, instead of paying him to stay on at the reception, request guests to take pictures for you. When negotiating with the photographer, agree that he would provide you with the digital pictures as well.

- Another tip for cutting the cost is to find an amateur photographer who is about to go professional and needs experience, ask friends and family you may be surprised who they know. Contacting photography colleges may be a good starting point.

- If you have guests coming with children, you can make up small bags for each child with things to keep them occupied. You may also include in each bag a disposable camera.

My Experience

We hired a photographer for the morning only, and we agreed that he would take about 20 formal pictures. We had a mock cutting of the cake (as the "real" cake cutting was scheduled for later on in the day). The pictures for the day cost us about £200.

We made the mistake of not negotiating up-front on the wedding pictures and getting the CD as part of their service. So the photographer charged us another £150 to get our pictures unto a CD.

Please don't make the same mistake!! Negotiate up-front so that you can keep the digital photos as well.

5.3.16 Transport

Hiring a Mercedes will typically cost you about £250 or more for 3 hours. Here are some alternatives.

- Check with family members or friends if they have special cars.
- You can also search for your local wedding hire car company.

My Experience

We decided to hire the car. We looked on the Yellow pages for a hire car company and found one with a chauffeur which cost us £200 for 3 hours. That was a bit more than we had expected.

5.3.17 The Video

Depending on the importance you attach to the video, you can choose to have it professionally done. Alternatively, you can get as many friends as possible to take videos, and then spend some time to edit it.

In my view, a videographer is a good idea to ensure you have one video at least which is of a professional quality!

My Experience

We chose not to have a videographer and we instead requested people to take videos of the ceremony and reception. With the benefit of hindsight, I would have gone for a videographer, to ensure we have one video which is of excellent quality.

5.3.18 Hen night and stag do

There are many ideas for Hen nights, which will not break the bank for yourself or your friends. Here are a few ideas, which should be passed on to the bridesmaid.

- Have a bridal shower. The person with the biggest living room hosts the party. Get some food, drinks and play games together. It is a great opportunity for the bride to receive nice presents and play naughty games.

- Check "top table" out and look for their special offers and group outing ideas: www.toptable.co.uk

5.3.19 Honeymoon

The average couple spends £2828 on a honeymoon, but a little creativity can get you something unforgettable for as little as £500. Here are some ideas:

- Rent a romantic cottage far from the crowd somewhere in the UK.
- Consider low cost flights plus a discounted hotel in a romantic European city.
- Check the special offers (or deals) section of the following sites:
    - www.expedia.co.uk
    - www.lastminute.com
    - www.opodo.co.uk
    - www.quovadistravel.co.uk
    - http://www.trailfinders.co.uk
- Go on your honeymoon during the low season, you will save a fortune. Avoid July-August, Christmas and New Year period, Easter break and Valentine's Day.
- Hire a cottage in any part of the UK.
- For wedding gifts, ask for holiday vouchers! These can be obtained from selected travel agents. Here are a few companies that offer holiday vouchers:
    - http://www.kuoni.co.uk/vouchers/index.shtml
    - http://www.thomson.co.uk/po/showEssentials.do?essential=vouchers

- When you are on honeymoon, do not hesitate to inform the hotel staff that you are on honeymoon; you would be surprised at the treatment that you will get. It is better to mention this to the company directly rather than the agent.

- http://www.quovadistravel.co.uk: They will personalise your honeymoon to your taste and you can get good discounts as well.

My Experience

We used lastminute.com and went on honeymoon in early December (before the Christmas rush). We got a deal for 7 nights in a 5* Hotel in Cyprus near Paphos.

On checking in, we told the Hotel reception that we were on honeymoon and they immediately upgraded us to a fantastic room with a sea view. We were offered 2 bottles of champagne and free gift vouchers to attend the spa. The honeymoon cost us £800 plus £200 spending money.

5.3.20 Gift lists

A gift list allows you to select the gifts you would like to receive. This will avoid received two of the same items.

Here are a few ideas for your wedding gift list:

- Register your list with a big superstore such as John Lewis, Debenhams as they are more likely to have constant stock, than your local gift shop.

- Rather than asking for presents for your house, you could ask for travel vouchers, as explained in the previous session.

- If you want to take the opportunity of a wedding to give back to charity, you can set up a gift list with charities. Here are some charities you could use:

    - http://www.cancerresearchuk.org/donate/give_in_celebration/

    - www.giveit.co.uk

5.3.21 Next steps

This section is only applicable if you have purchased the wedding planning tools. If you have not purchased it, you may do so by clicking on the following link:

http://www.weddingforless.co.uk/index.php/wedding-planner-tool.html

- You will need to go through the wedding items list and allocate an amount of money for each of the wedding items.
- Once that is done, you will need to go to the Wedding planning checklist worksheet and the groom's checklist. These lists are in chronological order so you can follow the given order.
- This can be used as a "to do" list, and you may put in additional tasks if necessary.
- Indicate a time frame for completing the various tasks
- You can now start shopping around and buying all the items that you need for your wedding...

6. PURCHASING YOUR ITEMS

6.1 TIPS ON NEGOTIATING

Negotiating is a skill, but with practice, anyone could become a master negotiator. I don't want to turn you into an expert negotiator overnight, but would like to give you some guidelines that will help you achieve a deal.

- Think about the transaction as 'give and take'. By this I mean that there must usually be something to be gained by the company in exchange for a discount. For example, if you are hiring the wedding car, and it costs £250 for 3 hours, you might say something like 'we'll offer you £200 and pay for the item in full now'. Or you could also try 'we'll offer £200 and we'll place the order now'.

- If your wedding ceremony and/or reception will be held at a hotel, ask for discounts when your family and friends are staying at the same hotel. Reserve a block of rooms for your guests several months before the wedding in order to get the best rates.

- Always speak with the appropriate manager when asking for discounts, as the Manager will be in a better position to offer discounts.

- Pick the right time to negotiate. If you are trying to negotiate in a peak season, your vendor might ignore you, as he knows that he can easily find another buyer. If it is in the low season, you are more likely to get a discount as the vendors will be looking for your business.

- Do not hesitate to tell vendors that you are on a budget, and ask them what they can offer for your maximum amount.

- If you have a number of alternatives, you will find yourself in a stronger bargaining position. For example, if you have found a venue with a site fee of 300 pounds and you have found another venue that you prefer with a site fee of 500 pounds. You could say: "I have found another venue which costs 300 pounds for the site fee, but I much prefer your location and would be ready to pay for it, but your site fee is above our budget. What can you offer us?"

- Try to hide your excitement and enthusiasm about items you have fallen in love with. A company will be less likely to respond to a request for a discount if they feel that their product is your only choice.

- Try to establish through conversation how busy your supplier is around the date of your wedding. At certain times of the year (October to May), companies can be very quiet so they will want your order (and money) as much as you want their products!

- Try to give the impression that there are products from other companies you are seriously considering but for a discount you are prepared to place an order now.

- Avoid showing too much interest or emotion. If you act too interested, the vendor will know that you have got you and they will pay premium prices. So try to hide your excitement and show that you are in charge.

- Finally, bear in mind that you generally get what you pay for. If you are a skilful buyer and you knock a company's price down too much, you may not get the full quality of service offered to those who are paying the full price. Companies need to make profit in order to stay in business, so don't insult them by offering too low a figure - a little saving is better than none at all. Remember, a good deal is when both parties are happy with the transaction.

6.2 QUOTATIONS AND ESTIMATES

Here are some tips on getting quotations and estimates:

- Be aware that there is a big difference between getting a quote from a company and getting an estimate. A quotation is a fixed price given by a company for the product or service you wish to buy, i.e. it is a legally binding contract between you and the supplying company. An estimate is what a company feels it should charge for the product or service, which may be different from what you end up paying.

- When drawing up your provisional budget, by all means ask for an estimate so you can get a feel for the general level of expenditure required. However, when you are in a position to place an order, always get a written quotation first. You must also ensure that you know exactly what the quotation is made up of, particularly what is and what isn't included.

- Before you place an order, try to get at least one or two other quote(s) so you see that you are paying a reasonable price for the goods or services offered. In many cases, this will not be possible, especially where you are considering items that are unique in some way. However, you should still try to satisfy yourself that you are getting value for money. If you are able to get an alternative quotation, always ensure that you are comparing like for like, otherwise your comparison will be meaningless.

- Also note, when requesting for quotations, some companies will charge VAT whereas others may not charge you VAT. You need to make sure that you have taken the VAT into account in your budgeting.

- Always ask about their policy for deposits. If the deposit is refundable, then you are fine, else DO NOT pay the deposit unless you are 100% sure that you will go for that product or service.

6.3 KEEPING TRACK OF YOUR EXPENSES

It is vitally important that you keep accurate records, particularly if you are working to a strict budget. You should keep all your paperwork, quotations and receipts you receive as well as details of any deposits paid and when any balances are due.

You can create a “wedding folder” where you would keep all quotations, receipts and paperwork related to your wedding costs.

7. POST-WEDDING ACTIVITIES

7.1 WHO TO TELL ABOUT YOUR NAME CHANGE

I have listed below many of the companies and organisations you need to advise of your change of name.

1. Employer.
2. Inland Revenue (obtain your reference and address from your employer).
3. Department of Health & Social Security (write to the Contributions Agency at your local Social Security Office).
4. Doctor.
5. Dentist.
6. DVLC.
7. Passport Office
8. Bank.
9. Building Society (mortgage and/or savings accounts).
10. Credit Card and Store Charge-Card Companies.
11. Finance/Loan Companies.
12. Premium Bond Office.
13. Investment Companies.
14. Companies that you have Shares in.
15. Pension Company.

16. Insurance Companies (e.g. motor, medical, life, property, property contents etc).

17. Mail-Order Catalogue Companies.

18. Motoring Organisations.

19. Professional Institutes and Bodies.

20. Clubs, Societies and Associations.

21. Internet Service Provider (if your e-mail address incorporates your old name, you may wish to change your e-mail address).

I have also provided a sample letter that you may wish to use when writing to the above organisations. Text between the braces {} is for your own details while the square brackets [ ] show optional text.

{your address}
{date}

{addressee}

Dear Sirs,[Account No.] [Policy No.] [National Insurance No.] [Ref No.]

I wish to advise you that following my [marriage on {date}] [change of name by Deed Poll on {date}], my name has changed from {previous name} to {new name}. Please amend your records accordingly.

I have enclosed a copy of my [marriage certificate] [Deed Poll]. Please let me know if you would like to see the original document or require any further information.

Yours faithfully,

{sign using your new name}
{print your new name}

The source of this information is: http://www.weddingguide.co.uk/articles/legal/changingnameadvise.asp

8. FINAL WORDS FROM LILLIAN

Have a wonderful day! It doesn't matter where you get married or what you do, just so long as you're marrying the person you love.

One thing I will say is, remember to relax and enjoy the day. Try as hard as possible to leave your 'party planner' role behind as you leave for the church and adopt the 'bride and 'groom'roles, which everyone is going to love!

Also, make sure you get as many photos from your guests as possible

Wishing you all the best on your special day!

Lillian

9. SOURCE OF INFORMATION

The following sources were used to compile this book or referenced in this document. Further useful information can be found on their websites:

Sources used to compile this book:

- www.confetti.co.uk
- www.hitched.co.uk
- www.moneysavingexpert.com/family/cheaper-weddings
- "Fire your wedding planner" by Stephi Stewart.

Wedding cakes:

- www.marksandspencer.co.uk
- www.tesco.com
- www.asda.co.uk
- www.charactercreations.co.uk

Dresses:

- www.debenhams.co.uk
- www.johnlewis.co.uk
- www.houseoffraser.co.uk

- www.coast-stores.com
- www.marksandspencer.co.uk
- www.bhs.co.uk
- www.theweddingdress.co.uk
- www.thebridalwearcompany.com
- www.sharethedream.co.uk
- www.almostnewweddingdresses.co.uk
- http://www.hitched.co.uk/sale
- www.oxfam.co.uk
- www.ebay.co.uk

Suit for groom:

- www.mossbroshire.co.uk
- www.youngs-hire.co.uk
- www.hire-society.com

Wedding rings:

- www.argos.co.uk
- www.weddingringworkshop.co.uk

Dresses for flower girls/page boys:

- www.redoute.co.uk

- www.vertbaudet.co.uk

Wedding Hair:

- http://www.weddinghair.com
- http://www.youandyourwedding.co.uk

Stationary:

- http://www.thepapermillshop.co.uk
- http://www.weddingcrafter.co.uk
- www.whsmith.co.uk
- www.clintoncards.co.uk/
- www.istockphoto.com

Hen night/stag do:

- www.toptable.co.uk

Honeymoon:

- www.expedia.co.uk
- www.lastminute.com
- www.opodo.co.uk
- www.quovadistravel.co.uk
- www.tripadvisor.co.uk

- www.lastminute.com
- http://www.kuoni.co.uk/vouchers/index.shtml
- http://www.thomson.co.uk/po/showEssentials.do?essential=vouchers
- http://www.trailfinders.co.uk

Guest list:

- www.johnlewis.co.uk
- www.debenhams.co.uk

Giving through charities:

- http://www.cancerresearchuk.org/donate/give_in_celebration/
- www.giveit.co.uk

APPENDIX B: ***VIDEO AND PHOTO CHECKLIST***

B.1 PHOTOGRAPHY[i]

A good time to start looking for a photographer and/or videographer is about nine to twelve months in advance. Begin with recommendations from family and friends, looking through albums for quality, style and formats that you like. Criteria to keep in mind when interviewing photographers include:

1. Do the pictures have a sharp, crisp quality?

2. Can they do retouching? What about special effects?

3. Will there be an extra charge for the proofs?

4. How long do they keep the negatives?

5. Does the price quoted include the finished album?

6. Do you feel confident with the person and are you convinced that he will perform professionally, inconspicuously and deliver great pictures?

7. Check for a mix of shots that are technically good.

8. Look for the emotion the photo projects.

9. Is the person who is showing you the photos the same person who will be shooting your wedding?

10. Discuss costs. Work out a clear payment schedule, and obtain an itemized agreement that lists everything included in the package and the total cost.

11. Can he/she arrive early to capture last-minute preparations, moments with family members, and the little events that make the day complete?

12. Will he/she design your album for you?

13. Can you see the proofs Online? Will the web address be available to friends & family? Can you order online?

B.2 VIDEOGRAPHY[ii]

The best time to start looking for a videographer is about nine to twelve months in advance. Begin with recommendations from family and friends, looking through tapes for quality, style and formats that you like. As you view a tape with the videographer, look for pans and zooms. Are they smooth? Does the tape tell a story? Here are some questions to ask when interviewing videographers:

B.2.1 What Does The Video Package Include?

1. Unedited tape

2. Multi-camera

3. Montage of stills

4. Titles

5. Narration

6. Background music

7. Close-up shots

8. Interviews with family, wedding party, guests

9. Can interviews be interspersed throughout the tape?

10. Can your taping be serious or humorous? Are creative options available?

11. Discuss costs. Work out a clear payment schedule.

12. Obtain an itemized agreement that lists everything included in the package and the total cost.

13. How many tapes come with the package? What is the cost for extra tapes?

14. How is the tape packaged professionally? Does it have a case, album, printed labels?

15. Is a deposit required? If so, how much?

16. How many hours of shooting does the price include?

17. Can he/she arrive early to capture last-minute preparations, moments with family members and unexpected situations?

18. How is overtime handled?

19. Does the videographer keep the tape? If so, how long?

20. How early must reservations be made?

21. What is the cancellation policy?

22. Can you select the background music, and is there a wide selection to choose from?

B.2.2 Is Broadcast-Quality Editing Equipment Used?

23. What kind of camera equipment will be used? Is it consumer or commercial quality equipment?

24. What is the format? (Should be hi-8 or super VHS)

25. Will there be sufficient light available at the time and location of the ceremony?

26. Is the person who is showing you the videos the same person who will be shooting your wedding?

27. Make sure you know who is taping the wedding, and get it in writing.

28. Is the videographer familiar with the site you have selected?

29. What will the videographer's attire be?

One last note: both of you must feel confident that this videographer will perform professionally and inconspicuously, and deliver a great video.

APPENDIX C: ***QUESTIONS ON THE VENUE***

C.1 THE VENUE [iii]

1. Is your venue available on the required date?
2. Is your venue easy to find?
3. Is your venue licensed to carry out civil weddings
4. If you do hold a license for civil ceremonies, what authority do you come under and can you supply names and contact details for the registrar?
5. Will our wedding be the only wedding at your venue on our wedding day?
6. How many people can you accommodate?
7. How many car parking spaces are available?
8. Do you allow confetti to be thrown at the venue?
9. Do you allow candles to be lit in the reception room?
10. Do you allow professional firework displays at your venue?
11. What are the various options and costs for the use of your venue?

C.2 THE ROOM

1. Do you offer the option of a marquee?

2. Are there separate rooms provided for the wedding, reception, meal, evening reception, etc?

3. Is there a room provided for the use of "bride and groom' for the day?

4. Is there a dressing room that the bride and bridesmaids can use prior to the ceremony?

5. When can we start setting up the room in terms of decorating it with balloons, flowers, banners, etc? (Morning of wedding, day before, etc?)

6. If the evening reception is being held in a room that is being used for something else earlier in the day, do you require the DJ/Band to set-up their equipment beforehand?

7. Is there an area that could be used as a crèche, if needed?

8. Is there a quieter area for older guests to get away from the noise of a band/DJ

9. If rooms are available for overnight accommodation, how many?

10. What are the costs for overnight accommodation?

11. Is breakfast included?

12. What is the checkout time the following day?

13. Do you have a room where wedding presents can be stored until you are able to collect them and are you insured for any loss or damage to these presents?

C.3 EXTRA QUESTIONS

1. Do you have a Public Address (PA) system that can be used for speeches?

2. What facilities are available if the weather is poor?

3. What photographic locations are there?

4. Do you supply or can you recommend a DJ or Band?

5. Do you have special arrangements with, or details of local hotels for guests to stay at?

6. Do you have any arrangements with local cab companies that offer a reasonably priced and reliable service?

7. Is there any entertainment provided during the void between the afternoon and evening receptions (casino, magician, etc)?

8. What decoration do you supply for the reception?

9. If we begin to run late, how will your staff help us to ensure we are still able to make the most of our big day?

10. Can you recommend a videographer?

11. Can you recommend a photographer?

12. Is it OK for the photographer/videographer to visit the venue beforehand to get an idea of what they can expect on the day?

13. Can you recommend a company that can supply wedding cars?

14. What facilities do you provide for a videographer?

15. Can you recommend a good florist?

16. Can you recommend a company that can supply favours? Can you recommend a company that supplies decorative balloons?

APPENDIX D: THE CATERER[iv]

1. Make sure the caterer is licensed or you may be liable if something happens.

2. If outdoors, make sure they have refrigeration.

3. Find out how they dress.

4. What is the estimated cost per person for a seated dinner? Buffet? Cocktail reception? Open bar? What does the cost include?

5. What is the staff-to-guest ratio? (For seated meals, the ratio is usually one waiter to 8-10 guests.)

6. Have you worked at any prospective reception sites? Can you recommend other sites for weddings?

7. Do you have a set menu? Can the menu be modified?

8. Can the kitchen staff adhere to special dietary restrictions for some guests who may be diabetic, kosher, and vegetarian?

9. Do you have liability coverage - including liquor liability?

10. Can you supply me with a list of references? (Contact two.)

11. How much advance time is needed to confirm a reservation?

12. Can I arrange to view the catering of another wedding reception to check food display, service style, flow, organization? Can we arrange to taste foods on the menu you suggest?

13. Do you set the tables? Provide linens? Order floral arrangements? Coordinate the music?

14. What additional charges might be incurred other than the food, beverages, and rental of requested extras?

15. How much advance time will you need to set up?

16. Can you send me a confirmation letter including the wedding date and time, names of service help, tipping policy, decorating time, colour schemes, menu, cost per person?

17. Can I see available linens? What is the additional rental cost?

18. How much food is enough? (Ten to twelve hors d'oeuvres per person is adequate. With buffets, offer a choice of two entrées.)

19. Will the hors d'oeuvres be hand served or on a buffet?

20. How much do you charge for overtime and cancellation?

21. Can you give me a ceiling on anticipated menu price increases? (Caterers quote final prices 90 days prior to the wedding. Due to rising food costs, an increase might be 10 %.)

22. When will the wedding cake be delivered (if your caterer will provide you with one)? Is the cake cut by the banquet staff?

23. Can we go over placement of the head table - on a raised platform or floor level, dais or round table?

24. How many drinks does each bottle of liquor, champagne, provide? Is there an opening fee per bottle of champagne?

25. Will you feed the photographers, the musicians?

26. What is the guarantee requirement for number of guests?

27. When must I provide a final guest count?

28. Do you insist on doing all the catering?

29. Can you supply examples of suggested menus along with prices?

30. Do you include a cake stand and knife, if required?

31. Do you have a preferred order of service (when and where do we cut the cake)?

32. Until when do you offer an alcohol license?

33. By what time do you insist the reception be finished?

34. Do you insist on supplying the wine and champagne?

35. If we are able to supply the wine, what do you charge for corkage?

36. Can you recommend a company to supply our wedding cake?

APPENDIX E: ***LIST OF PHOTOGRAPHS TO TAKE***

This list[v] will ensure that you do not forget any photographs, whether they are taken by your friends or a professional photographer.

Before the Wedding

- [ ] Bride dressing for ceremony
- [ ] Bride, full-length solo
- [ ] Bride with parents
- [ ] Bride with mother/father separately
- [ ] Bride with sisters/brothers
- [ ] Bride with grandparents
- [ ] Bride with maid of honour
- [ ] Bride with attendants
- [ ] Bride with groomsmen
- [ ] Bride with ringbearer, flower girl

- [ ] Groom dressing for ceremony
- [ ] Groom, close-up
- [ ] Groom with mother/father separately
- [ ] Groom with sisters/brothers
- [ ] Groom with grandparents
- [ ] Groom with best man
- [ ] Groom with bridesmaids
- [ ] Groom with groomsmen
- [ ] Attendants getting ready

- Attendants outside church

During the Wedding

- Parents being seated
- Bridesmaids walking down aisle
- Flowergirl & Ringbearer walking down aisle
- Bride and father walking down aisle
- Father giving bride's hand to groom
- Exchanging of vows
- Breaking glass, jumping broom
- Unity Candle (becoming more popular)
- Soloists
- Readers
- Ring ceremony
- Kissing ceremony
- Recessional

Right After the Wedding

Formal bride and Groom together	Newlyweds with bride's immediate family
Newlyweds with parents	Newlyweds with bride's extended family
Newlyweds and	Newlyweds with

entire bridal party	groom's immediate family
☐ Newlyweds with minister/priest	☐ Newlyweds with groom's extended family

During the Reception

☐ Close-up of newlywed's rings	☐ Newlywed's first dance
☐ Cake table	☐ Father's last dance with daughter
☐ Cutting the cake	☐ Flower girl dancing with ringbearer
☐ Couple feeding cake to each other	☐ Guest dancing
☐ Best man toasting newlyweds	☐ Groom cutting the groom's cake.
☐ Best man and Groomsmen decorating the car	☐ Wedding party dance.
☐ Cake and punch servers	☐ Candid photos of the bride and groom having fun with their family and friends.
☐ Musicians / DJ	

Leaving the Reception Area

☐ Bride tossing bouquet	☐ Guests throwing rice, bubbles

☐ Someone catching the bouquet	☐ Newlyweds getting into car, limo or carriage
☐ Groom tossing garter	☐ Car, limo, carriage driving away
☐ Someone catching the garter	☐ Newlyweds waving goodbye
	☐ Guest waving goodbye

Additional photos

☐ Post-reception party	☐ Bride changing into going away cloths
☐ Exterior of wedding location	☐ Newlyweds leaving on honeymoon

---

More information can be found below:

i http://www.weddingorg.com/articles/weddingphotographertips.htm

ii http://www.weddingdetails.com/planning/photovid.cfm

iii www.hitched.co.uk/venues/questions.asp

iv http://www.weddingdetails.com/planning/caterer.cfm

www.ingramcontent.com/pod-product-compliance
Ingram Content Group UK Ltd.
Pitfield, Milton Keynes, MK11 3LW, UK
UKHW020236250726
13967UKWH00001B/406